HART PICTU
ARCHIVES

Designs of the
Ancient World

Compiled by Robert Sietsema

Hart Publishing Company, Inc. • New York City

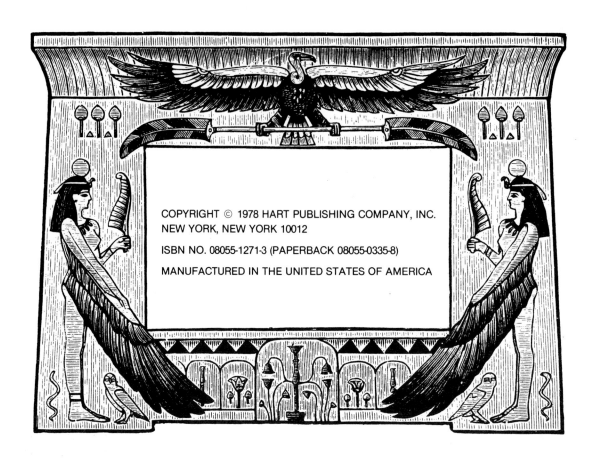

CONTENTS

HOW TO USE THIS BOOK

DESIGNS OF THE ANCIENT WORLD is a collection of over 250 pictures of many periods, culled from 25 known sources. These pictures have been subdivided into 6 categories.

All these pictures are in the public domain, and may be used for any purpose without fee or permission. Most of the pictures derive from books and magazines for which copyright is not in force. Others are copyrighted by Hart Publishing Company, but are now released to the public for general use.

So as not to clutter a caption, the source is given an abbreviated designation. Full publication data may be found in the *Sources* section, in which all sources are listed in alphabetical order, with the full title of the book or magazine, the publisher, and the date of publication. The *Sources* section commences on page 79.

Two of the pictures are halftones, and they are designated by a square symbol at the end of each caption. These pictures, too, are suitable for reproduction, but the user is alerted to rescreen such a picture or convert it into line. All other pictures can be reproduced directly in line.

Assyrian Designs

Border designs, two examples. *Hart Publishing*

Bas-relief. *L'Art, Vol. 24*

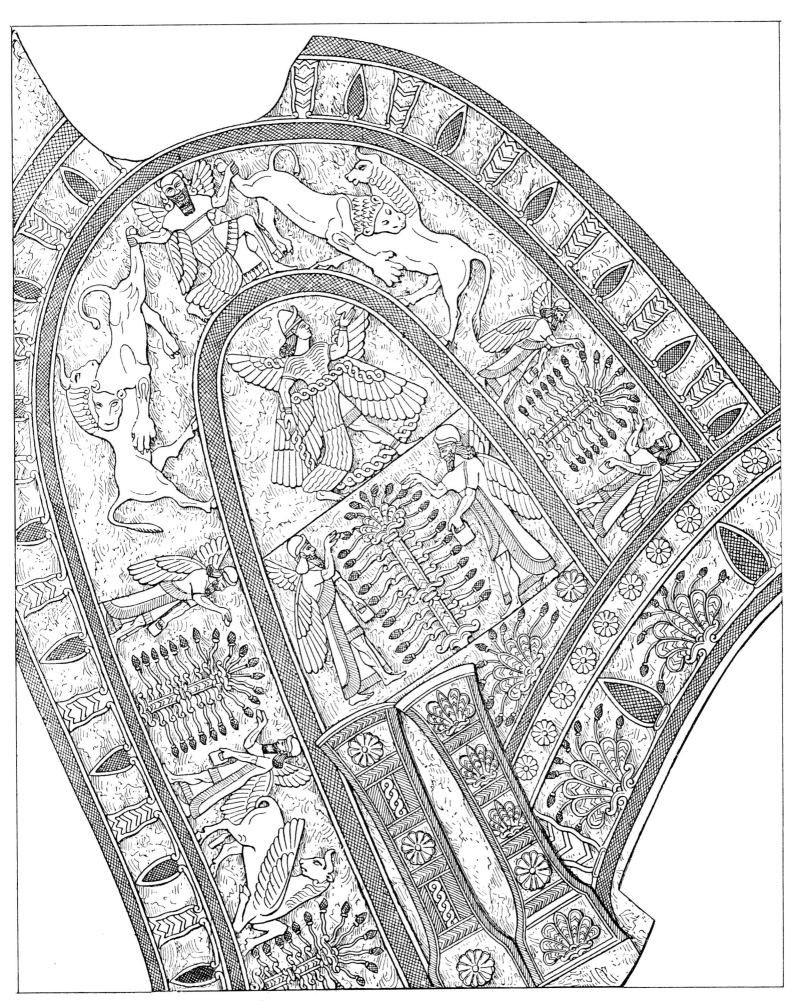

Embroidered mantle of a monarch. *Historic Ornament*

Assyrian Designs continued

Statue of a winged deity found at Nimrod, dating from 800 B.C. *London News, Vol. 17*

Foliage on a marble relief, circa 650 B.C. *L'Art, Vol. 13*

Assyrian court officials, from a relief. *Sunday Book*

Assyrian Designs continued

Hunting scene, bas-relief fragment. *L'Art, Vol. 21*

Bronze platter. *Historic Ornament*

Attire of a king. *La vie privee*

Winged bull from Nineveh. *Voyages & Travels, Vol. 1*

Coptic Designs

Textile design. *Coptic Textiles*

Embroidered ornament. *L'Art & Coptic Textiles*

Border design. *Coptic Textiles*

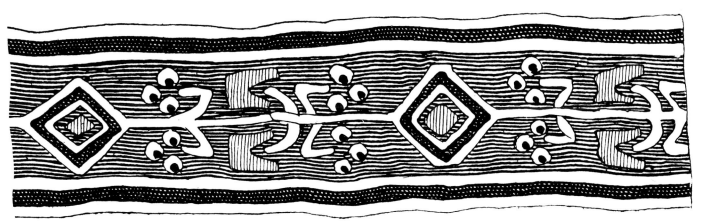

Border design. *Coptic Textiles*

Coptic Designs continued

Textile designs. *L'Art, Vols. 37 & 39*

Textile design. *Coptic Textiles*

Coptic embroidery. *L'Art, Vol. 40*

Egyptian Designs

Plants found in the Land of Punt. Carved in the temple at Deir-el-Bahari, circa 1500 B.C. *Pattern Design*

Temple painting. *Hart Publishing* □

Bird hunting in ancient Egypt, tomb painting. *L'Art, Vol. 21*

Egyptian Designs continued

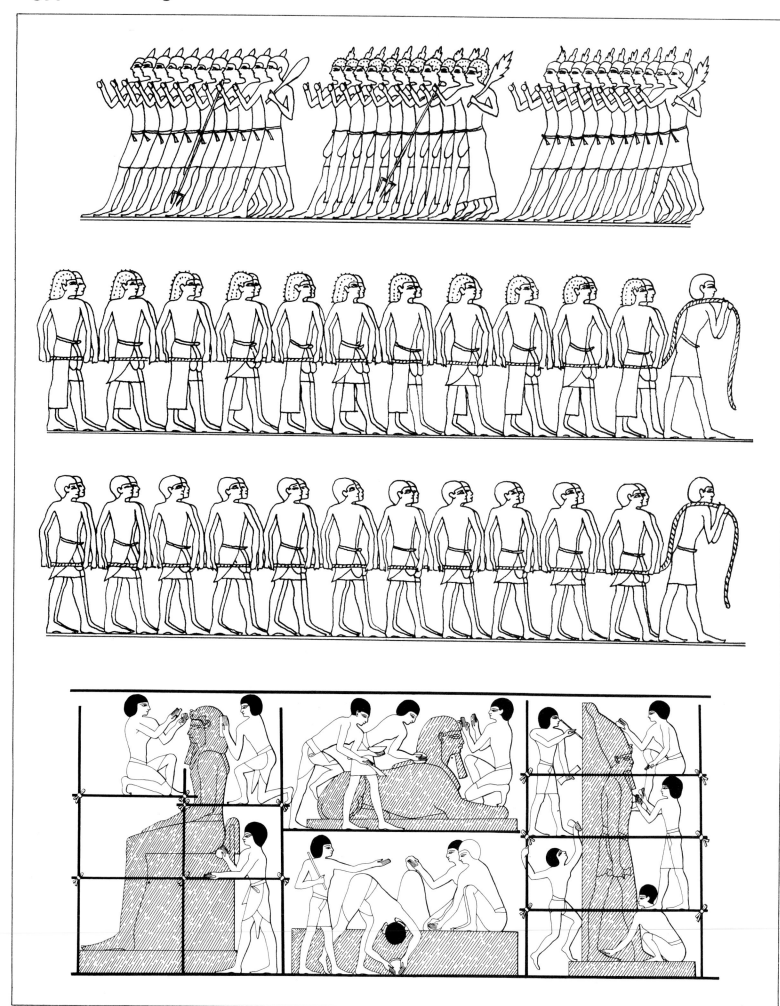

Workers sculpting and transporting monuments, depicted on tomb walls. *Century, Various Vols.*

Incarnations of Isis. *Source Illustrations*

Osiris enthroned. *Industrial Arts*

The cosmology. *Countries of the World*

Egyptian Designs continued

Monolith from the Temple of Philoe, with two border designs from the same temple. *L'Art, Vol. 16*

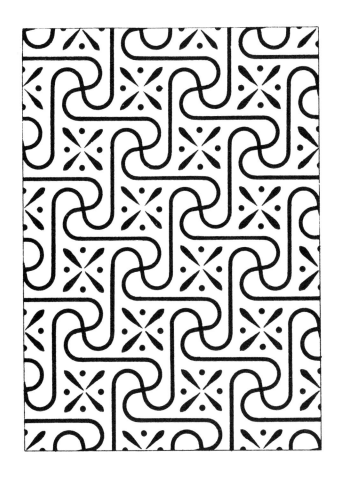

Diaper ornament. *Outlines*

Egyptian Designs continued

Painting of Anukeh and Ramses,
from an Egyptian temple. *Century, Vol. 13*

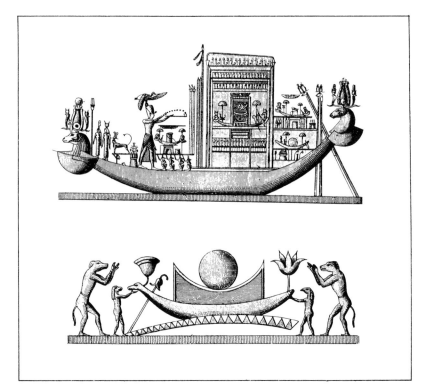

Sacred ships. *Source Illustrations*

Painting of a hawk. *Meyer's*

Ceremonial headdresses. *Costumes*

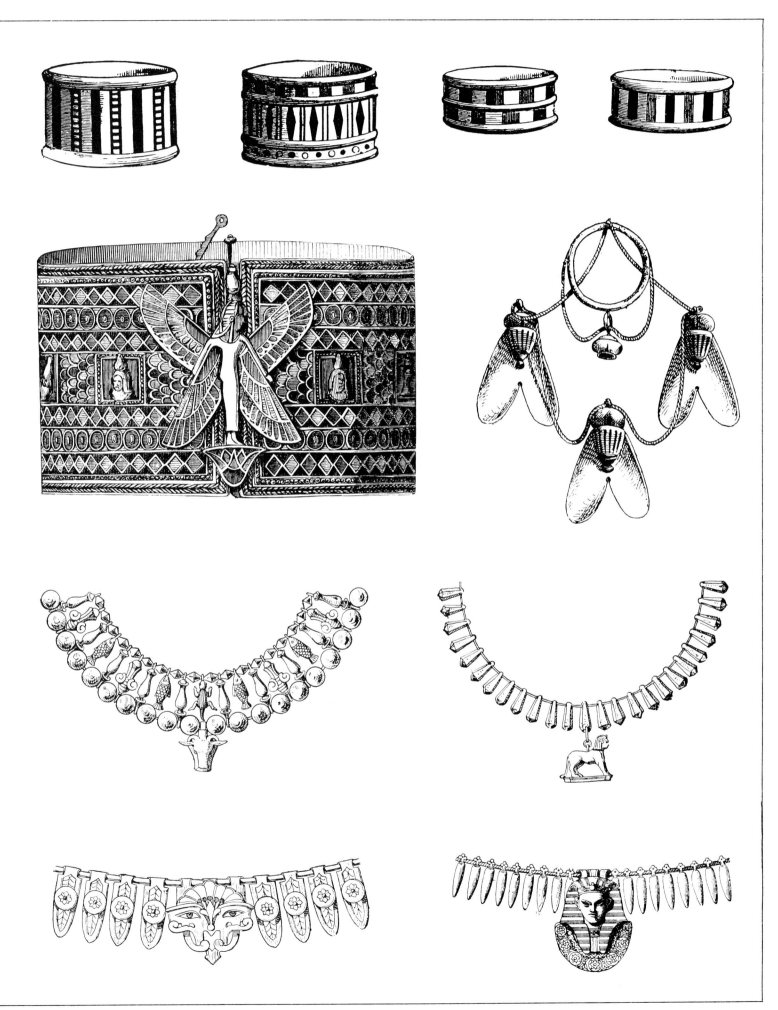

Egyptian jewelry. *Jewelry*

Egyptian Designs continued

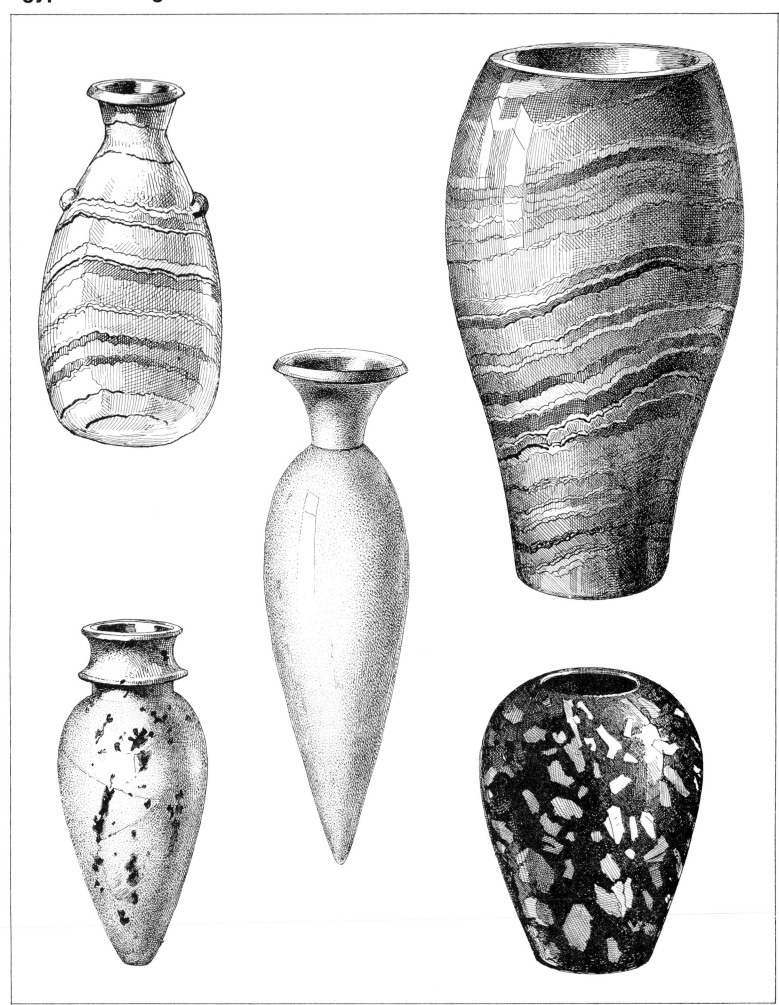

Apotheosis of Ramses II. The king is seated upon his throne while three gods (Amen-Ra-Tum, Safekh, and Tahut) are engaged in inscribing his name upon the fruits of the Tree of Life. *Century, Vol. 13*

Phoenician medallions. *Cyprus*

Apis, the sacred bull of Memphis. *Industrial Arts*

Egyptian Designs continued

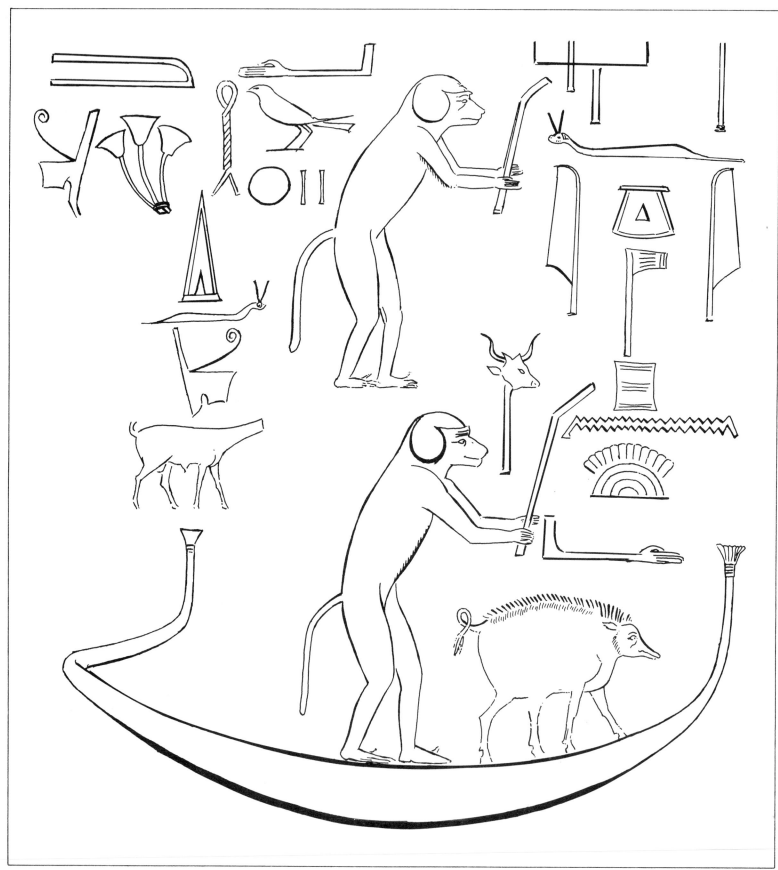

Tomb painting. *Hart Publishing*

Mural tablet at Gebel Silsilis. *Century, Vol. 38*

Frieze from the Temple of Denderah Tentyris. *L'Art, Vol. 16*

Egyptian Designs continued

Granite statue. *L'Art, Vol. 18*

Diaper ornament. *Outlines*

Various Egyptian designs. *Hart Publishing*

Greek Designs

Terra cotta ornament. *Gewerbehalle, Various Vols.*

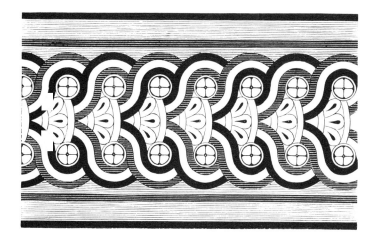

Terra cotta ornament. *Gewerbehalle, Various Vols.*

Greek Designs continued

Corinthian unguent bottles, shown actual size. *L'Art, Vols. 2 & 3*

Ancient Etruscan funery urn. *L'Art, Vol. 21*

Greek Designs continued

Painted dish. Details page right. *L'Art, Vol 16*

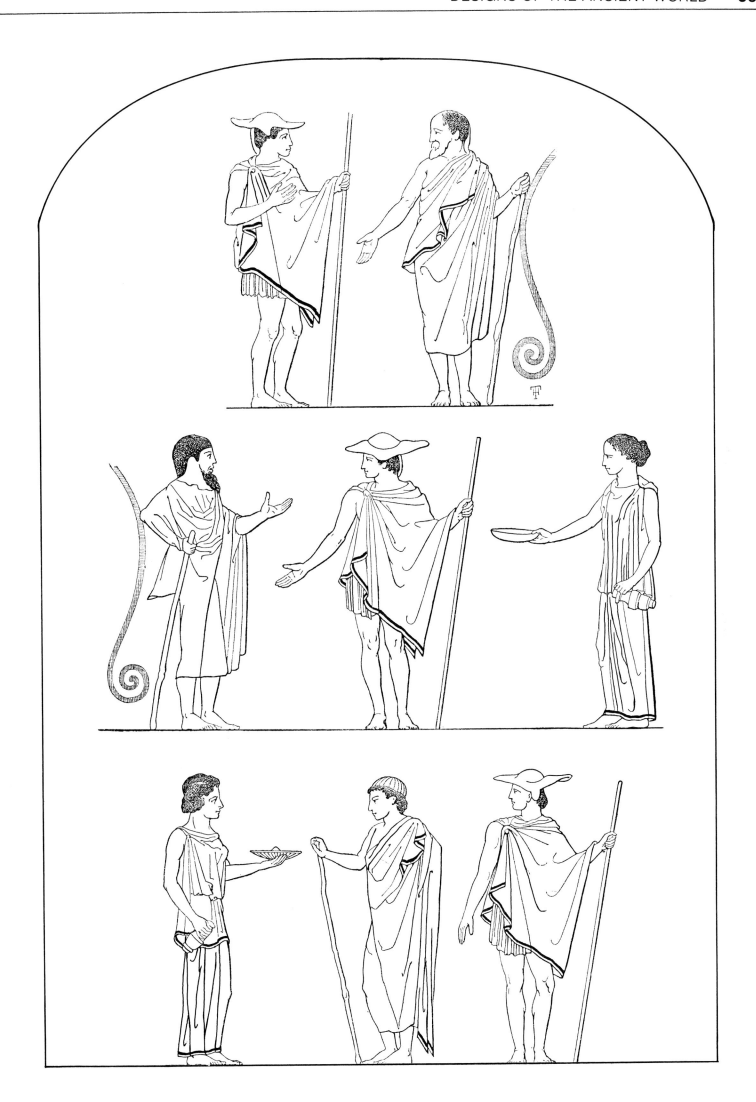

Greek Designs continued

Small painted dish, from the Louvre Museum. *L'Art. Vol. 23*

Terra cotta ornament, two examples. *Workshop, Vol. 2*

Greek Designs continued

Attire of Greek women. *Costumes*

Greek Designs continued

Terra cotta stele. *Gewerbehalle, Vol. 8*

Tragic masks carved in stone. *L'Art, Vol. 22*

Corinthian vase painting. *L'Art, Vol. 4*

Greek Designs continued

Terra cotta antefix, ornamented with a tragic mask. *Workshop, Vol. 12*

Design from the inside of a cup. *L'Art, Vol. 4*

Greek Designs continued

Fret ornament. *Outlines*

Vase design. *Gewerbehalle, Vol. 6*

Greek Designs continued

Etruscan design. *Gewerbehalle, Vol. 7*

Capital of pilasters in the Temple of Eleusis, at Athens. *Encyclopedia of Ornament*

Honeysuckle cornice stone. *Workshop, Vol. 6*

Greek Designs continued

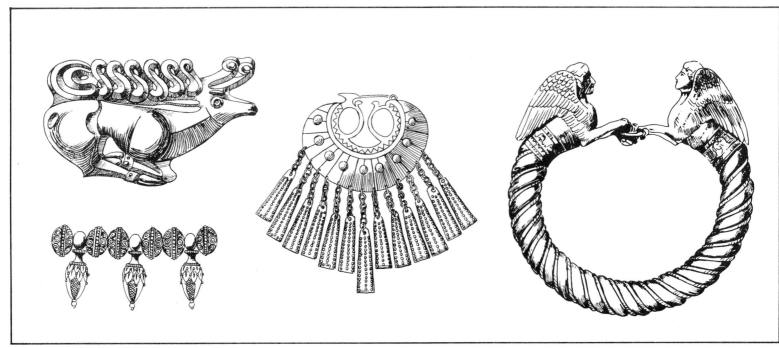

Ancient Greek jewelry. *Metiers d'Art*

Architectural ornament. *Gewerbehalle, Vol. 10*

Terra cotta fragment depicting the death of Penthesilea in the arms of Achilles. *L'Art. Vol. 4*

Greek Designs continued

Vase to be awarded at games, inscribed "Made by Andocides." *L'Art, Vol. 4*

Detail from vase at left, depicting female athletes preparing for racing and wrestling. *L'Art, Vol. 4*

Etruscan vase design. *Gewerbehalle, Vol. 8*

Greek Designs continued

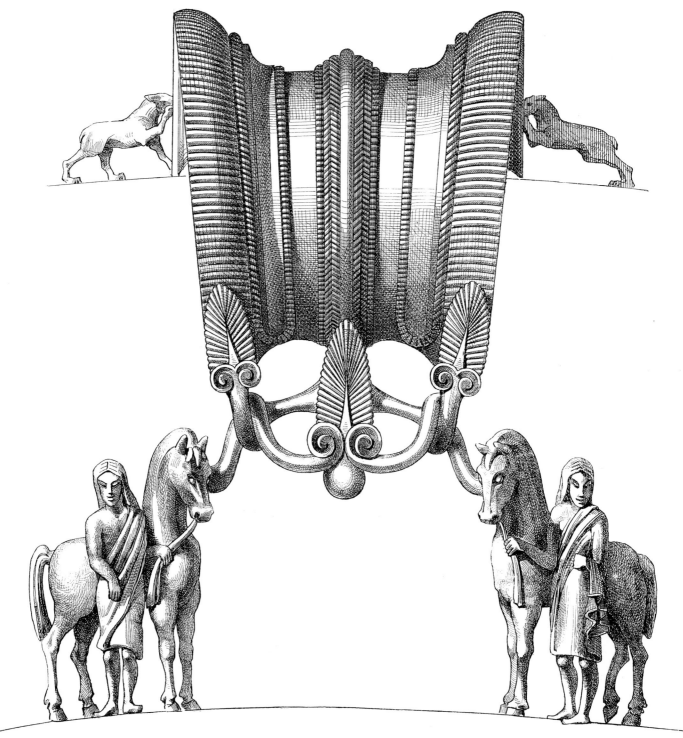

Bronze handle on an Etruscan vase. *L'Art, Vol. 12*

Grecian ceramic border of late date. *Workshop, Vol. 12*

Vase painting from the earliest epoch of Greek art. *Short History*

Cretan vase. *Pattern Design*

Mycenean vase. *Pattern Design*

Greek Designs continued

Bas-relief depicting the Curetti striking their shields in order to drown the wailings of the infant Jupiter. *L'Art, Vol. 9*

Various fans. *L'Art, Vol. 39*

Anthropomorphic rhytons. *L'Art, Vol. 26 & 27*

Roman Designs

Sarcophagus of Alexander Severus and Mamaea. *Roman People*

Border designs in terra cotta. *Workshop, Vol. 3*

Design on a drinking vessel. *Gewerbehalle, Vol. 5*

Roman Designs continued

Marble flower from the Forum of Nerva. *Gewerbehalle, Vol. 11*

Imperial Roman eagle, in marble. *Gewerbehalle, Vol. 4*

Cornice ornament in marble from the Temple of Jupiter Tonans. *Workshop, Vol. 10*

Roman Designs continued

Fragment from a frieze depicting Leda and the swan. *L'Art. Vol. 12*

Bull adorned for sacrifice. *Costumes*

Krater ornamented with laurel. *Gewerbehalle, Vol. 9*

Roman Designs continued

Dress of Roman generals. *Costumes*

Kraters engraved with ivy. *Workshop, Vol. 6*

Bronze mask of Bacchus, shown actual size. *L'Art, Vol. 22*

Roman Designs continued

Vase in the shape of a rhyton. *L'Art, Vol. 22*

Rosettes. *Workshop, Vol. 8*

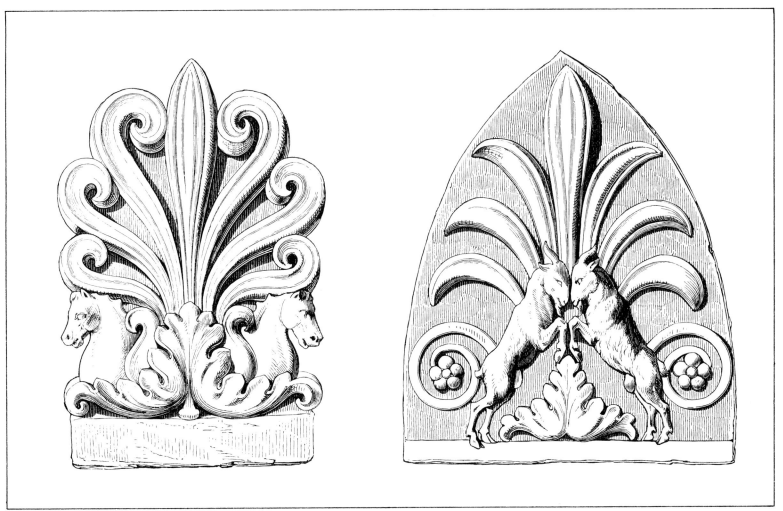

Terra cotta antefixes. *Gewerbehalle, Vol. 9*

Terra cotta frieze. *Workshop, Vol. 4*

Roman Designs continued

Silver vase. *L'Art, Vol. 21*

Marble statue of Augustus. *L'Art, Vol. 12*

Miscellaneous Designs

Saracenic embroidered silk. *L'Art, Vol. 34* ▫

Satin breastplate embroidered with gold, worn by
Jewish women. *L'Art, Vol. 17*

Miscellaneous Designs continued

Moorish designs. *Workshop, Vols. 10 & 17*

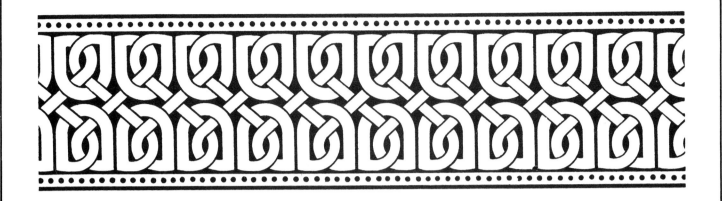

Celtic frets. *Outlines*

Miscellaneous Designs continued

Moorish engraved plate, made of silver. *L'Art, Vol. 16*

Arabic architectural ornament. *Workshop, Various Vols.*

Miscellaneous Designs continued

Ancient Cambodian relief depicting combat between an elephant and a lion with a human mask, from the palace at Angkor-Thom. *L'Art, Vol. 34*

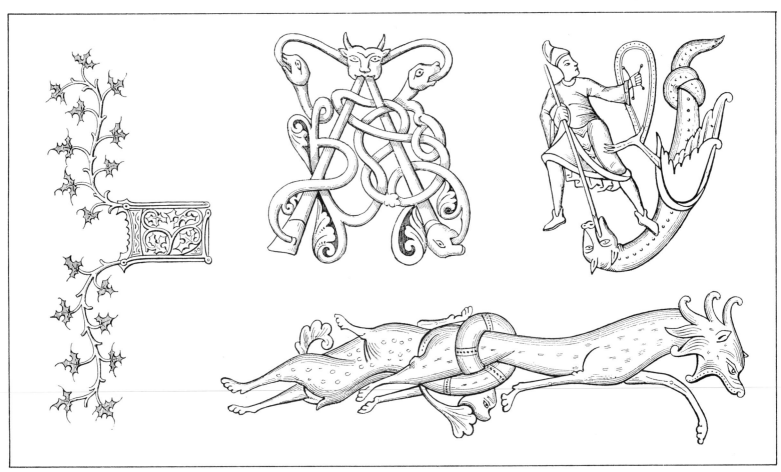

Byzantine manuscript ornament. *L'Art, Vol. 29*

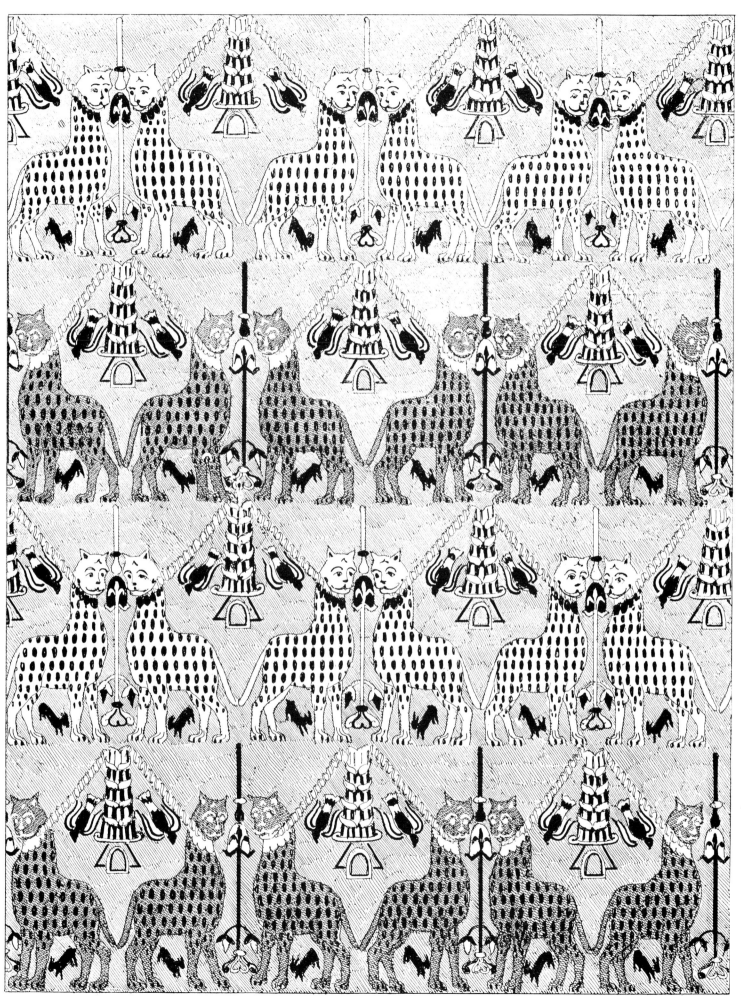

Persian fabric design depicting leopards guarding the sacred altar while looking at the tree of life. *L'Art, Vol. 24*

Miscellaneous Designs continued

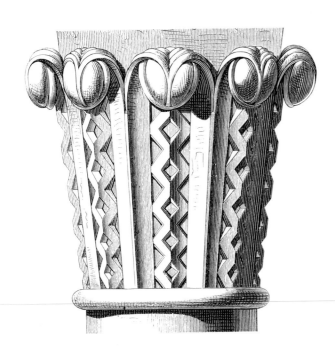

Romanesque capitals. *Workshop, Various Vols.*

French Romanesque architectural ornament. *Gewerbehalle, Vol. 4*

SOURCES

CENTURY; full title, *The Century Illustrated Monthly Magazine.* New York: The Century Company, 1883-1901.

COPTIC TEXTILES; full title, *Coptic Textile Designs.* Gerspach, M. New York: Dover Publications, 1975.

COSTUMES; full title, *Costumes of the Greeks and Romans.* Hope, Thomas. New York: Dover Publications, 1962.

COUNTRIES OF THE WORLD (six vols.). Brown, Robert. London: Cassell and Company, Ltd., n.d.

CYPRUS; full title, *Cyprus; Its Ancient Cities, Tombs, and Temples.* Cesnola, Luigi Palma di. New York: Harper, 1878.

ENCYCLOPEDIA OF ORNAMENT. Shaw, Henry. Edinburgh: 1842.

ENCYCLOPEDIA OF SOURCE ILLUSTRATIONS. Heck, J.G., ed. London: Morgan & Morgan, 1972.

GEWERBEHALLE: *Organ fur den Fortschritt in allen Zweigen der Kunst-Industrie.* Schnorr, Julius, ed. Vienna: 1862-1883.

HART PUBLISHING COMPANY; Original illustrations by Hart Publishing Company artists.

HISTORIC ORNAMENT (two vols.). Ward, James. London: Chapman & Hall, 1897.

INDUSTRIAL ARTS; full title, *Chefs-D'Oeuvre of the Industrial Arts.* Burty, Phillipe. New York: D. Appleton & Co., 1869.

IOUIYA & TOUIYOU; full title, *The Tomb of Iouiya and Touiyou.* Davis, Theo. M. London: A. Constable, 1907.

JEWELRY. Sietsema, Robert. New York: Hart Publishing Company, 1978.

L'ART; full title, *L'Art Pour Tous, Encyclopedie de l'Art Industriel et Decoratif.* Reiber, Emile, ed. Paris: A. Morel et C., 1861-1906.

LA VIE PRIVEE; full title, *La vie privee des anciens* (four vols.). Paris: Morel, 1880-1883.

LONDON NEWS; full title, *Illustrated London News.* London: George C. Leighton, 1866-1900.

METIERS D'ART; full title, *Histoire des meiers d'art.* Fontanes, Jean de. Paris: n.d.

MEYERS; full title, *Meyers konnerlations-Lexikon.* Leipsig und Wein: Bibliographisches Institut, 1895.

OUTLINES; full title, *Outlines of Ornament in the Leading Styles.* Audsley, W.&G. New York: Scribner, 1882.

PATTERN DESIGN. Christie, Archibald H. New York: Dover Publications, 1967.

ROMAN PEOPLE; full title, *History of Rome and of the Roman People From Its Origin to the Invasion of the Barbarians.* Boston: Estes & Lauriat, 1890.

SHORT HISTORY; full title, *A Short History of Art.* De Forest, A. & Julia B. New York: Phillips & Hunt, 1881.

SUNDAY BOOK; full title, *The Pictorial Sunday Book.* Kitto, Dr. John, ed. London: The London Printing and Publishing Company, Ltd., n.d.

VOYAGES AND TRAVELS (2 vols.). Calange. The Walker Co., n.d.

WORKSHOP, THE: *A Monthly Journal, Devoted to Progess of the Useful Arts,* (English language edition of *Gewerbehalle*). Baumer, W., and J. Schnorr, eds. New York: E. Steiger, 1868-1883.

HART PICTURE ARCHIVES

TITLES IN PREPARATION